Searchlight
BOOKS™

Do You
Know the
Continents?

Learning
about
Europe

Roberta Baxter

Lerner Publications • Minneapolis

Content Consultant: Corey Johnson, Associate Professor, Department of Geography, The University of North Carolina–Greensboro

Lerner Publications Company
A division of Lerner Publishing Group, Inc.
241 First Avenue North
Minneapolis, MN 55401 USA

For reading levels and more information, look up this title at www.lernerbooks.com.

Library of Congress Cataloging-in-Publication Data

Baxter, Roberta, 1952–
        Learning about Europe / by Roberta Baxter.
            pages cm. — (Searchlight books. Do you know the continents?)
        Includes index.
        Audience: Grades 4 to 6.
        ISBN 978-1-4677-8019-3 (lb : alk. paper) — ISBN 978-1-4677-8351-4
    (pb : alk. paper) — ISBN 978-1-4677-8352-1 (eb pdf)
            1. Europe—Juvenile literature. I. Title.
    D1051.B38 2015
    940—dc23   2015000987

Manufactured in the United States of America
1 – VP – 7/15/15

Contents

Chapter 1

THE CONTINENT OF EUROPE

Europe is the second-smallest continent. Only Australia is smaller. But more than seven hundred million people live in Europe. That makes it the continent with the third-highest population. How can that be? Europe has a high population density. This means that many Europeans live very close together.

Many people live close to one another in European cities. How many people live in Europe?

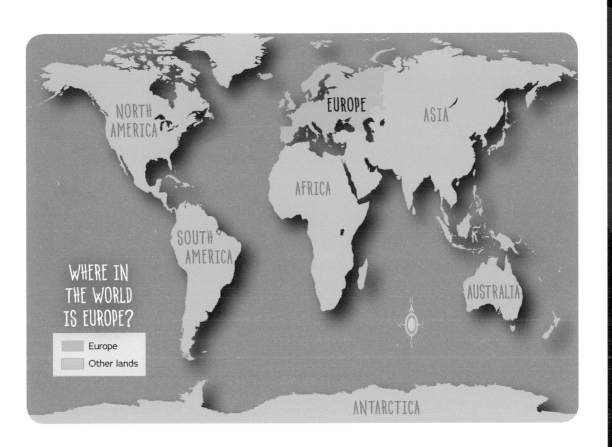

WHERE IN THE WORLD IS EUROPE?

- Europe
- Other lands

NORTH AMERICA

SOUTH AMERICA

EUROPE

ASIA

AFRICA

AUSTRALIA

ANTARCTICA

EUROPE SHARES A LONG BORDER
WITH ASIA TO THE EAST.

The tallest mountains of the Urals are smaller than Asia's highest peaks, yet the Urals still reach high into the sky.

Natural Borders

Europe's western part touches the Atlantic Ocean. The Mediterranean Sea divides the continent from Africa in the south. Europe's northern areas, including Russia, touch the Arctic Ocean.

Most continents are divided from other continents by oceans. Europe's border with Asia is different. The Ural Mountains separate Europe and Asia. Because of this, some geographers do not consider Europe a separate continent. They instead call the combined landmass Eurasia.

Common History

Europe has about fifty countries. The number isn't exact because some lie partly in Europe and partly in Asia. Experts disagree about which continent they belong to.

Though Europe has many nations, the continent's people have much in common. They share a past shaped by Europe's ancient peoples. They visit one another's countries. Many nations even share the same money!

Most residents of Europe can travel freely between the continent's countries.

Chapter 2

COUNTRIES AND CITIES

Greece and Rome are important cultural centers in Europe. These countries were major civilizations in ancient times. The Greeks were powerful in the 400s and 300s BCE. They lived around the Mediterranean Sea. The Romans came later. Their empire was centered on Rome, Italy. They ruled until the 400s CE.

Many ancient Greek buildings are still standing. Where did the ancient Greeks live?

France, England, Portugal, and Spain were major world powers too. These nations came to power in the 1500s. They sent ships to explore the world's oceans.

PORTUGUESE EXPLORER FERDINAND MAGELLAN LED A VOYAGE AROUND THE WORLD IN THE EARLY 1500s.

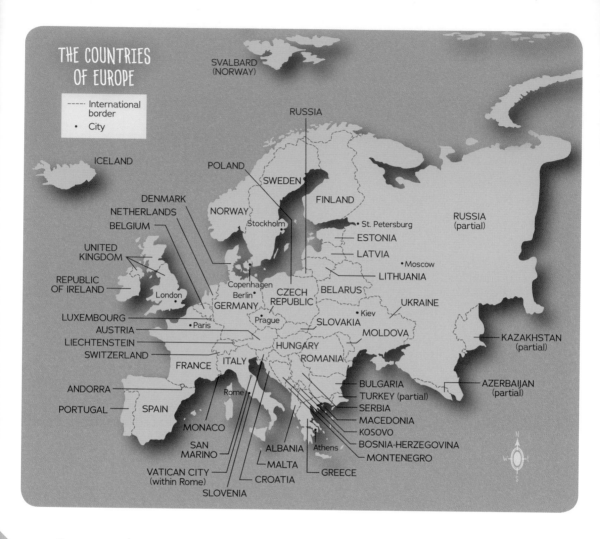

THE COUNTRIES OF EUROPE

----- International border
• City

SVALBARD (NORWAY)

RUSSIA

ICELAND

POLAND

SWEDEN

DENMARK

NETHERLANDS

BELGIUM

NORWAY

Stockholm

FINLAND

RUSSIA (partial)

• St. Petersburg

ESTONIA

LATVIA

• Moscow

LITHUANIA

UNITED KINGDOM

REPUBLIC OF IRELAND

London

Copenhagen

Berlin•

GERMANY

CZECH REPUBLIC

BELARUS

UKRAINE

LUXEMBOURG

AUSTRIA

LIECHTENSTEIN

SWITZERLAND

• Paris

Prague

SLOVAKIA

• Kiev

MOLDOVA

KAZAKHSTAN (partial)

FRANCE

ITALY

HUNGARY

ROMANIA

ANDORRA

PORTUGAL

SPAIN

Rome•

BULGARIA

TURKEY (partial)

SERBIA

MACEDONIA

KOSOVO

AZERBAIJAN (partial)

MONACO

SAN MARINO

ALBANIA

Athens

BOSNIA-HERZEGOVINA

MONTENEGRO

VATICAN CITY (within Rome)

MALTA

CROATIA

GREECE

SLOVENIA

Huge and Tiny Countries

Russia is another major player in Europe's cultural life. It is the world's biggest country in land area. With about 140 million people, Russia also has the largest population of any European country. The relatively large nation of Germany is in second place. More than 80 million people live there.

The world's smallest country is called Vatican City. It is within the city of Rome. Vatican City takes up only 0.17 square miles (0.44 square kilometers). That is about the size of a golf course! About eight hundred people live in Vatican City. The Roman Catholic Church is based there.

MILLIONS OF PEOPLE VISIT SAINT PETER'S SQUARE IN VATICAN CITY EACH YEAR.

Nineteen European Union countries used the euro as their money in 2015.

The European Union

Europe's many diverse nations created the European Union (EU) in 1993. By 2015, twenty-eight countries had joined. The group promotes peace on the continent. It also encourages trade. Most EU countries share a currency. It is called the euro.

Big and Beautiful Cities

In addition to its many countries, Europe is home to famous and fascinating cities. Russia's capital is Moscow. It is the continent's largest city. More than eleven million people live there. Its churches are known for their onion-shaped domes. Another major city is London, England. It has more than eight million people. A famous clock in London is nicknamed Big Ben. Many tourists come to see it.

Big Ben (RIGHT) is a popular London attraction.

Ancient Wonders

Many European cities are very old. Some buildings in Athens, Greece, are more than three thousand years old! The Colosseum in Rome was built between about 69 and 79 CE. The Golden Gate is found in Kiev, Ukraine. It was built about one thousand years ago.

Europe is full of history. You can hear classical music in Vienna, Austria. You can row through the watery canals of Venice, Italy. Or you can explore stone castles in the Czech Republic. What European nations and cities would you like to visit?

The Golden Gate was heavily damaged over the years. Workers restored and repaired it in the late 1900s.

European Artists

Several European countries were home to very famous artists, including sculptors, painters, writers, and composers. For example, Michelangelo, an artist from what is now Italy, made beautiful marble sculptures. Painter Leonardo da Vinci, also from Italy, created the *Mona Lisa* (BELOW), a famous painting that is in the Louvre Museum in Paris, France. Notable European writers include William Shakespeare, of England, and Leo Tolstoy, of Russia. The composers Wolfgang Amadeus Mozart and Ludwig van Beethoven were from modern-day Austria and Germany, respectively.

Chapter 3

LANDFORMS AND CLIMATE

Plains cover western Europe. The southern and eastern parts of the continent have high mountain ranges. They include the Alps, the Caucasus, and the Urals. The Alps are popular with climbers and skiers. Unlike all the other continents, Europe has no large deserts.

The plains of Germany have homes and farms. What type of landform is not found in Europe?

Warm Waters

The warm Mediterranean Sea gives southern Europe a comfortable climate. It makes Greece and Italy good places to grow crops. Many islands fill the Mediterranean Sea. Crete and Sicily are two of the largest.

THE WEATHER ON MEDITERRANEAN ISLANDS IS OFTEN SUNNY AND WARM.

The North Atlantic Current flows through the Atlantic Ocean. It carries warm water from Florida to Europe. The current heats up western Europe. This makes the weather mild. The United Kingdom is as far north as Canada. But the current keeps it much warmer.

Ocean currents help British people enjoy more warm-weather days.

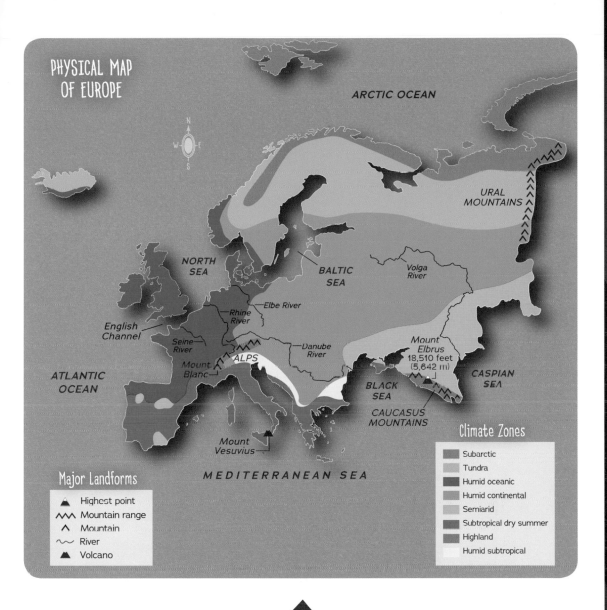

PHYSICAL MAP OF EUROPE

ARCTIC OCEAN

URAL MOUNTAINS

NORTH SEA

BALTIC SEA

Volga River

Elbe River

Rhine River

English Channel

Seine River

Danube River

Mount Elbrus 18,510 feet (5,642 m)

CASPIAN SEA

ATLANTIC OCEAN

Mount Blanc

ALPS

BLACK SEA

CAUCASUS MOUNTAINS

Mount Vesuvius

MEDITERRANEAN SEA

Major Landforms

▲ Highest point
ᴧᴧᴧ Mountain range
ᴧ Mountain
〜 River
▲ Volcano

Climate Zones

■ Subarctic
■ Tundra
■ Humid oceanic
■ Humid continental
■ Semiarid
■ Subtropical dry summer
■ Highland
□ Humid subtropical

WHAT IS EUROPE'S MOST COMMON CLIMATE ZONE?

Cold Countries

Norway, Sweden, Finland, and Russia are far to the north. They are cold and snowy. Few people live in the northern parts of these countries. Their southern areas are warmer. More people live there.

NORTHERN EUROPE RECEIVES
HEAVY SNOW IN THE WINTER.

European Volcanoes

Mount Vesuvius is a volcano in Italy. Its most famous eruption happened in 79 CE. The volcano destroyed the ancient Roman city of Pompeii. Mud and ash covered the city. The most recent eruption was in 1944. Iceland also has volcanoes. This island nation is in the North Atlantic Ocean.

Chapter 4

NATURAL RESOURCES

Europe has a wealth of natural resources. Its wide forests are filled with animals. Its waters contain many kinds of fish. And crops grow all over the continent.

Europe's forests are rich with natural resources. What kinds of resources are found there?

Forests

Northern Europe has large forests. The trees there can survive cold weather. They include spruce and pine trees. Central Europe's forests have leaves that fall off each autumn. Trees such as ash and oak fill these forests. Cork and olive trees are common in the Mediterranean region.

EUROPEANS HAVE HARVESTED OLIVES FOR THOUSANDS OF YEARS.

Foxes can survive winters in Europe's snowy forests.

Animals

Europe's animals vary by region. Elk and brown bears live in the north. Foxes and wolves prowl in central Europe's forests. Dolphins splash in the Mediterranean Sea. Falcons, finches, and ravens fly through the skies.

Other animals live on nature reserves. One is Hortobágy National Park in eastern Hungary. It is the largest grassland in Europe. Water buffalo and sheep live there.

FARMERS HAVE RAISED ANIMALS ON THE GRASSLANDS OF EASTERN HUNGARY FOR THOUSANDS OF YEARS.

Nature in Danger

Europe's forests were once much larger. But people cut down trees to make space for cities. They used the wood to build structures. They also overhunted many animals. Later, people began working to protect Europe's natural resources.

Huge forests have been cut down throughout Europe.

White Cliffs of Dover

The famous white cliffs of Dover are in the United Kingdom. They tower over the English Channel. This body of water separates the United Kingdom from France. The channel is only about 21 miles (33 km) wide in some parts. The cliffs of Dover are made of chalk. They can be seen from miles away.

Chapter 5

PEOPLE AND CULTURES

Europe has many different peoples. There are more than 160 cultural groups. They speak many languages. Each group has its own traditions. They have a wide variety of religious beliefs as well.

Signs in Europe often include many languages. How many cultural groups does Europe have?

EUROOPA PARLAMENT

ΕΥΡΩΠΑΪΚΟ ΚΟΙΝΟΒΟΥΛ

EUROPEAN PARLIAMEN

PARLEMENT EUROP

PARLAIMINT NA h

Languages

Many European languages are Romance languages. They come from the Latin language. The ancient Romans used Latin. Major Romance languages include Spanish and French. Other languages are Germanic. They include German and English. Many people in eastern Europe speak Slavic languages. Russian and Polish are two common Slavic languages.

> **The Russian language is written using Cyrillic letters. Many of these letters differ from the English alphabet.**

More than twenty thousand people participate in La Tomatina.

Festivals

Many different festivals are held throughout Europe. One of the most famous is La Tomatina in Spain. It is a huge food fight! People throw tomatoes at one another for fun. The festival has taken place since 1945.

Religion

Roman Catholicism is one of Europe's major religions. Many Catholics live in western Europe. Protestants are common in northern Europe. Eastern Orthodox Christians live in eastern Europe.

Large numbers of Europe's Jewish people died during World War II (1939–1945). This was due to the Holocaust, the killing of millions of Jews by the Nazis, a German political party. Other Jewish people left after the war. Still, many Jews now live in Europe. The continent also has many Muslims, or people who follow the Islamic faith.

The Pope

The leader of the Roman Catholic Church is called the pope. When a pope dies or resigns, church officials choose a new one. They hold a meeting called a conclave. It takes place in the Sistine Chapel in Vatican City. This historic church was built in the 1400s. The officials vote for a new pope. White smoke comes from the roof when a new pope is chosen. Pope Francis became the pope in March 2013.

Chapter 6

ECONOMICS

Europe has a diverse economy. Its mines contain valuable minerals. European companies are famous for technology and fashion. And Europe's farms produce a wide variety of food.

A beautiful stone called marble is found in Europe. Besides mining, what other industries are part of Europe's economy?

Minerals and Energy

European mines produce metals such as titanium and silver. A mineral called feldspar is used in pottery and tile. It is also used in glass.

European countries get fossil fuels from the ground. Scotland produces oil. Norway produces natural gas.

Europeans also use clean energy. These energy sources create less pollution than fossil fuels. Windmills collect energy from the wind. Solar panels turn the sun's rays into electricity.

Huge structures are used to get oil from under the ground.

European Industries

Many companies in Europe make cars. Car companies such as BMW and Ferrari are based in Europe. France and Italy are known for fashion. Switzerland's banking industry is famous. The country is also famous for chocolate and cheese. Italy grows olives and grapes. Tourism is important too. People from around the world visit Europe to enjoy its culture and history.

FERRARI, BASED IN EUROPE, IS KNOWN FOR ITS FAST, EXPENSIVE CARS.

WHERE ARE GRAPES GROWN?
WHY MIGHT THEY GROW IN
THESE PLACES BUT NOT OTHERS?

▼

NATURAL RESOURCES
OF EUROPE

Wheat
Cheese
Olives
Grapes
Wool
Titanium
Silver
Feldspar
Oil
Natural
gas

----- International
border

Protecting Resources

Some of Europe's natural resources are running out. Governments work to protect these resources. They have taken steps to stop overfishing. They have made laws to protect forests.

A United Continent

Europe is a diverse continent. It has big cities, forests, and farms. Its people speak many languages. They follow different customs. Europe has many historic cities to explore. Where will your European adventure begin?

Amazing landscapes and a rich history can be found in Europe.

Exploring Europe

Choose two or three places in the map above that you want to know more about. Choose places from different parts of Europe. Research these places online. What unique things are there to see and do? What do people eat? What local celebrations or festivals take place there? Write a paragraph about a trip that you will take to each place. What will you see and do?

Glossary

canal: a human-made waterway on which boats travel

composer: a person who writes music

conclave: a meeting at which a new pope is chosen

currency: the type of money used in a particular country or area

current: a flow of water

empire: a large area of land controlled by a single nation or ruler

geographer: a scientist who studies Earth

nature reserve: a place where people protect threatened plants or animals

population density: the average number of people in a given area

Expand learning beyond the printed book. Download free, complementary educational resources for this book from our website, www.lerneresource.com.

Learn More about Europe

Books

Doeden, Matt. *Tools and Treasures of Ancient Greece*. Minneapolis: Lerner Publications, 2014. Learn about one of the ancient cultures that continues to shape modern Europe.

Newman, Sandra. *Europe*. New York: Children's Press, 2009. In this book, you can read more about Europe's history, culture, and geography.

Woods, Mary B., and Michael Woods. *Seven Natural Wonders of Europe*. Minneapolis: Twenty-First Century Books, 2009. Explore the natural places that make Europe an exciting place to visit.

Websites

EU Kids' Corner
http://europa.eu/kids-corner/index_en.htm
Learn about what the EU does and how it works using games, quizzes, and interactive activities.

European History
http://history.howstuffworks.com/european-history
Take a look at this site to explore European history.

Interactive Europe Map
http://mrnussbaum.com/world/europe
Click this interactive map to show facts about European countries.

Index

Photo Acknowledgments

The images in this book are used with the permission of: © Tupungato/Shutterstock Images, p. 4; © Laura Westlund/Independent Picture Service, pp. 5, 10, 19, 35, 37; © Alex Ischenko/iStockphoto, p. 6; © Michele Tantussi/Getty Images, p. 7; © arssecreta/iStockphoto, p. 8; © North Wind Picture Archives, p. 9; © DNY59/iStockphoto, p. 11; © Mistika S./iStockphoto, p. 12; © Kamira/Shutterstock Images, p. 13; © Nickolay Vinokurov/Shutterstock Images, p. 14; © Theresa Scarbrough/Shutterstock Images, p. 15; © riekephotos/Shutterstock Images, p. 16; © imagIN.gr photography/Shutterstock Images, p. 17; © N K/Shutterstock Images, p. 18; © Robin Eriksson/iStockphoto, p. 20; © lrescigno/iStockphoto, p. 21; © Vlada Z./Shutterstock Images, p. 22; © Risteski Goce/Shutterstock Images, p. 23; © Jaroslav Moravcik/Shutterstock Images, p. 24; © Attila Jandi/Shutterstock Images, p. 25; © salajean/Shutterstock Images, p. 26; © asmithers/iStockphoto, p. 27; © Symbiot/Shutterstock Images, p. 28; © jcarillet/iStockphoto, p. 29; © Alberto Saiz/AP Images, p. 30; © neneos/iStockphoto, p. 31; © Nneirda/iStockphoto, p. 32; © V. Belov/Shutterstock Images, p. 33; © Somatuscani/iStockphoto, p. 34; © Vaclav Volrab/Shutterstock Images, p. 36.

Cover image: © Planet Observer/Universal Images via Getty Images.

Main body text set in Adrianna Regular 14/20.
Typeface provided by Chank.